TUNNEL
THE ARCHAEOLOGY OF CROSSRAIL

Tunnel: The Archaeology of Crossrail

This edition published in the United Kingdom in 2017
by Crossrail Limited: 25 Canada Square,
Canary Wharf, London, E14 5LQ.

Text © Crossrail Limited 2017
Design & Layout © Crossrail Limited 2017

ISBN 978-0-9933433-2-2

Author: Jackie Keily
Editor: Sarah Allen
Contributor: Jay Carver
Art Direction & Design: Andrew Briffett

With additional contributions from
Museum of London, Crossrail and its partners

Crossrail Limited is registered in England and Wales
No. 4212657.
Registered Office:
25 Canada Square, Canary Wharf, London, E14 5LQ.

TUNNEL

THE ARCHAEOLOGY OF CROSSRAIL

Sir Terry Morgan CBE, Chairman of Crossrail

"The story of London uncovered from beneath the streets of the city will be one of the greatest legacies of the Crossrail project, to be enjoyed for years to come."

With thanks to our partners: Transport for London (TfL), London Underground Limited (LUL), Network Rail, Historic England, Canary Wharf Group, City of London Corporation, Berkeley Homes, Museum of London Archaeology (MOLA), Oxford Archaeology, Museum of London and the Natural History Museum.

Foreword from Sharon Ament, Director of the Museum of London

The Museum of London, across our venues in the City and in Docklands, tells the ever-changing story of this great world city and the people who live here. Our galleries, exhibitions, displays and activities give you a sense of the vibrancy that makes London such a unique place.

The construction of London's newest railway, which will be known as the Elizabeth line when services begin in 2018, has given archaeologists a unique chance to explore some of the city's most historically important sites. Since work began in 2009, the project has undertaken one of the most extensive archaeological programmes ever in the UK, with over 10,000 artefacts shining a light on almost every important period of the Capital's history.

From east to west, the Crossrail project has dug through layers of London's rich history, unearthing a wealth of fascinating stories and objects. The Tunnel exhibition takes us on a journey from prehistoric forests and marshes to the marvels of 21st century engineering. It includes objects illustrating the human history of London, from Mesolithic times over 8,000 years ago, to the 20th century. Crossrail has enabled us to discover new and exciting stories of London and we are proud to have worked with them to deliver this exciting exhibition.

Foreword from Andrew Wolstenholme OBE, Chief Executive Officer, Crossrail

By 2030 the capital's population is set to reach ten million and its transport system must be ready to meet this demand. The railway that Crossrail is building – to be known as the Elizabeth line from 2018 – is part of part of the UK's plan to maintain London's place as a world-class city.

The new railway will be a high frequency, high capacity service linking 40 stations over 100 kilometres, from Reading and Heathrow in the west to Shenfield and Abbey Wood in the east. It will reduce congestion by increasing central London's rail capacity by 10 per cent. It will create new routes into and through the city, giving 1.5 million additional people access to central London within 45 minutes. It will improve journey times and deliver an accessible, world class experience for the travelling public.

To deliver this new railway, Crossrail needed to build ten new stations, transform eight existing stations and upgrade another 22. These new stations, with improved public realm and developments above, will be linked by 42 kilometres of new tunnels under London and improved railway infrastructure to the east and west of the route.

The scale of this project, reminiscent of the great engineering endeavours of Brunel - some of whose railway works were uncovered west of Paddington - represented a unique opportunity to learn about the history of the city. Woven into the project from the start, archaeological investigations were planned amongst the many miles tunnelled beneath the city and the excavation of over 40 construction sites. Over 10,000 objects were uncovered from prehistory to the present day. Reporting and analysis of these items has contributed to our understanding of the past, from early geological changes, to the habits of Roman London, the DNA of the Black Death and the great Plague and beyond.

Public interest in our archaeological finds has been served by public lectures, viewing platforms, community digs, video footage and media interest. This book, along with the Archaeology Series which analyses each major site in detail and the finds themselves, deposited with partners including the Museum of London and the Natural History Museum represents a lasting resource for all those fascinated by the history of London.

This archaeological resource is part of the legacy of a historic project. Alongside the wildlife habitats created by spoil from construction sites, the many engineers trained in specialist underground construction skills, the hundreds of apprentices in the industry who started their careers with Crossrail – these wider benefits will continue to add value long after the railway is open. From the end of 2018, passengers will be able to travel through the new central London tunnels and stations of the Elizabeth line and marvel at the finds discovered along the way.

Crossrail and London's archaeology

Crossrail is building the Elizabeth line, a new railway that will open, in phases, from 2018. It covers some 118 kilometres, running from Abbey Wood and Shenfield in the east, through the heart of London's West End, to Heathrow and Reading in the west. This book takes you on a journey under London, following the construction of the Elizabeth line from east to west. Along the way you will dig deep into London's past and uncover the amazing archaeological discoveries of the Crossrail project.

Building a new train line under London presented many challenges and required innovative engineering techniques. Forty two kilometres of tunnels had to be dug under some of London's busiest streets, avoiding building foundations, underground lines, water pipes and electrical cabling. This is why most of the tunnels were dug between 30 and 40 metres below ground. Ten new stations were built to serve the line and 30 more existing stations were upgraded.

Most of the tunnels were too deep to disturb the archaeology. However, where new stations and structures were built, where the tunnels reached the surface (the portals), or where the line connected with existing stations, there was the unique opportunity to uncover layers of London's history. From the very beginning, archaeology was a priority – to excavate, record and communicate what was found along the route and add to our knowledge about the history of the capital.

From prehistoric forests and marshes to marvels of 21st century engineering, the twin threads of archaeology and engineering were drawn together in a project that has pushed boundaries and broadened knowledge. Over 200 archaeologists worked on the project over a period of about fourteen years and and tens of thousands of artefacts were recovered.

From east to west this book contains nine chapters highlighting the most exciting archaeological discoveries made during the Crossrail project.

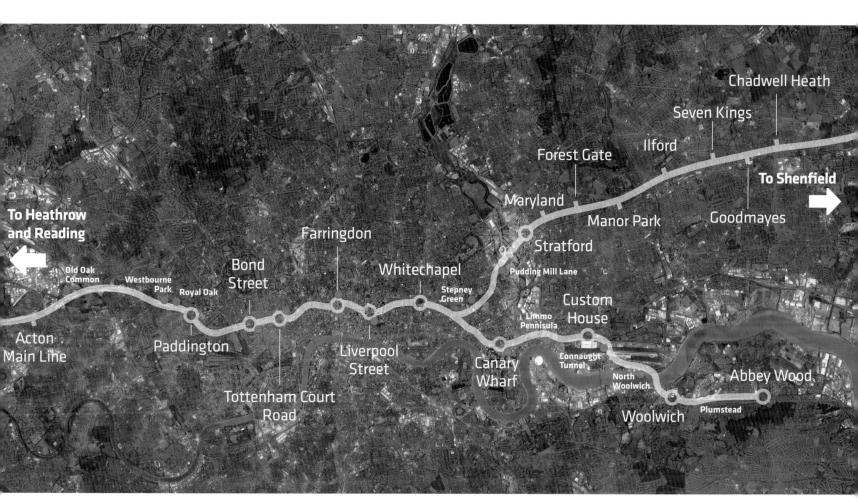

To Heathrow and Reading ←

Acton Main Line
Old Oak Common
Westbourne Park
Royal Oak
Paddington
Bond Street
Tottenham Court Road
Farringdon
Liverpool Street
Whitechapel
Stepney Green
Canary Wharf
Limmo Pennisula
Custom House
Connaught Tunnel
North Woolwich
Woolwich
Plumstead
Abbey Wood
Pudding Mill Lane
Stratford
Maryland
Forest Gate
Manor Park
Ilford
Seven Kings
Goodmayes
Chadwell Heath

To Shenfield →

Major Crossrail archaeology sites ●

Archaeology on the Crossrail project

In an infrastructure project the size of Crossrail, with 40 work sites and construction planned above and below ground over a route of 118 kilometres, the potential for archaeological discovery, recording and analysis was significant. From the early stages of the project's inception, the design of an archaeology programme to maximise the findings along the route was planned to work in harmony with large scale construction.

As early as 2004, bore holes were dug along the project's route, to determine geological conditions. These samples were used to help validate the planned railway route and confirm the methodology and machinery required for building the new tunnels, stations and shafts. The data was also used to plan ways of protecting the ground from movement during tunnelling and to assess the target sites for archaeological excavation.

Where construction would take place at or close to deposit of potentially rich archaeological interest, trial pits were dug, sometimes in streets or through the floors of existing buildings, to investigate what was there. Of all Crossrail worksites in London and the South East, 30 needed trial pits to establish their archaeological value. Analysis of these led to the planning of 20 extensive excavations. At some sites, archaeologists were able to excavate prior to building work beginning, but at most they needed to work side by side with engineers, planning their investigations to fit in with the digging of huge holes in the ground and the construction of tunnels, stations, shafts and portals.

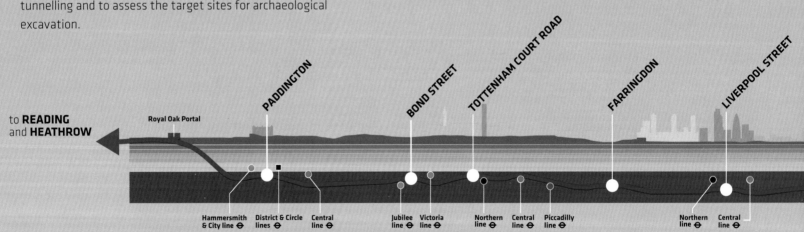

to **READING** and **HEATHROW**

Royal Oak Portal

PADDINGTON

BOND STREET

TOTTENHAM COURT ROAD

FARRINGDON

LIVERPOOL STREET

Hammersmith & City line ⊖ District & Circle lines ⊖ Central line ⊖ Jubilee line ⊖ Victoria line ⊖ Northern line ⊖ Central line ⊖ Piccadilly line ⊖ Northern line ⊖ Central line ⊖

Diagram shown not to scale

Archaeology in London is usually found within the top nine metres below ground level.

Most of the train tunnels are much deeper than this, often 30 to 40 metres below ground. The archaeology was therefore mainly found during the building of new stations which are not as deep, where other forms of surface work was taking place, where grout shafts were excavated to help stabilise the surrounding land and at the portals, where the larger tunnels surfaced.

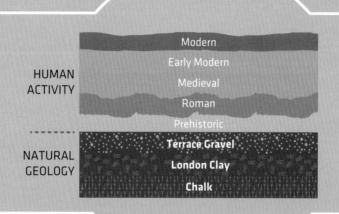

HUMAN ACTIVITY

Modern
Early Modern
Medieval
Roman
Prehistoric

NATURAL GEOLOGY

Terrace Gravel
London Clay
Chalk

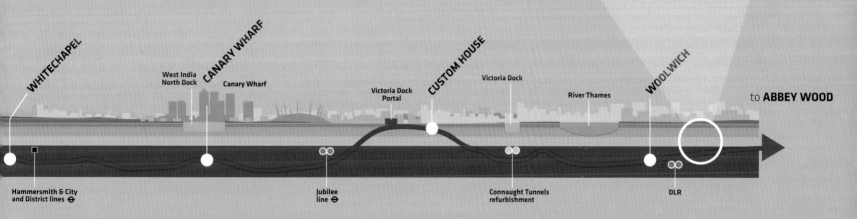

WHITECHAPEL

Hammersmith & City and District lines

West India North Dock

CANARY WHARF

Canary Wharf

Jubilee line

Victoria Dock Portal

CUSTOM HOUSE

Victoria Dock

Connaught Tunnels refurbishment

River Thames

WOOLWICH

DLR

to **ABBEY WOOD**

Tunnel Boring Machines

Eight giant machines were used to make the tunnels for the train line. Called tunnel boring machines (TBMs), they were used in pairs to create two tunnels, one for the eastbound trains and one for the westbound, along the central part of the route. Some of the most amazing moments of the project were when these gigantic machines broke through to join the tunnels and stations together.

Each TBM was given a woman's name, following mining traditions:

Sophia and Mary

The tunnels from Plumstead to North Woolwich were bored by two TBMs called Sophia and Mary. Sophia was named after the wife of Marc Isambard Brunel who built the first tunnel under the Thames. Mary was named after the wife of their son, the famous 19th century railway engineer Isambard Kingdom Brunel.

Victoria and Elizabeth

The tunnels from the Limmo Peninsula to Farringdon were bored by two TBMs called Victoria and Elizabeth, after Queen Victoria and Queen Elizabeth II.

Jessica and Ellie

The tunnels from Pudding Mill Lane to Stepney Green (and also from Victoria Dock to the Limmo Peninsula) were bored by two TBMs called Jessica and Ellie. They were named after Olympic heptathlon champion Dame Jessica Ennis-Hill DBE and Paralympic swimming star Ellie Simmonds OBE. The names were chosen by students at the Marion Richardson Primary School in Stepney. These were the only two machines to bore two separate tunnels each.

Ada and Phyllis

The tunnels from Farringdon to Royal Oak were bored by Ada and Phyllis. These TBMs were named after Ada Lovelace, the world's first computer programmer, and Phyllis Pearsall, who created the London A-Z.

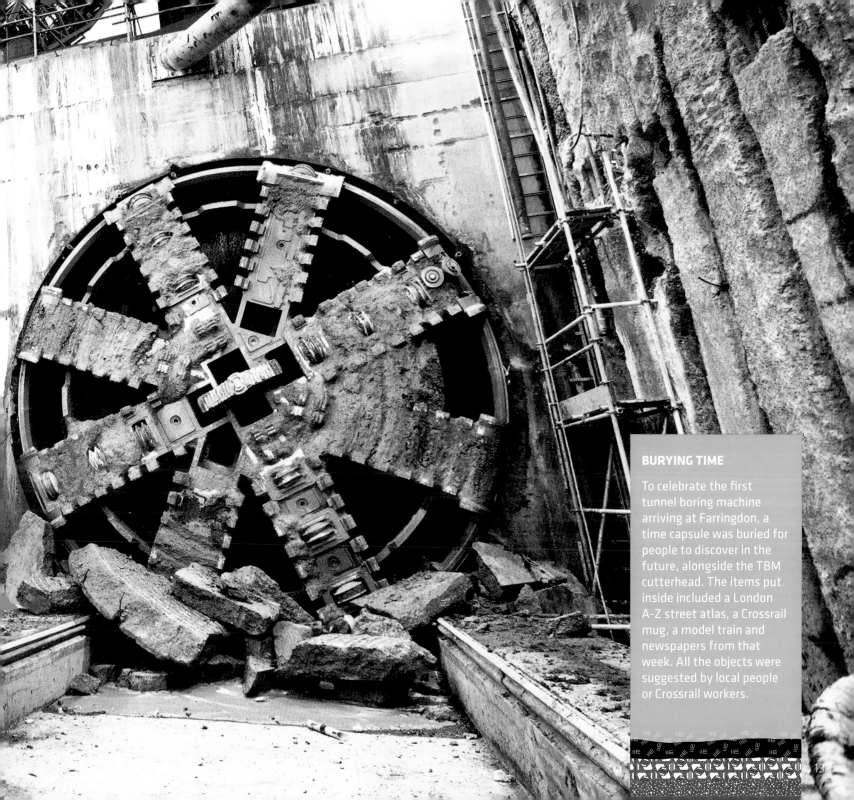

BURYING TIME

To celebrate the first tunnel boring machine arriving at Farringdon, a time capsule was buried for people to discover in the future, alongside the TBM cutterhead. The items put inside included a London A-Z street atlas, a Crossrail mug, a model train and newspapers from that week. All the objects were suggested by local people or Crossrail workers.

London through the ages

The size and population of London has changed dramatically over time. Founded by the Romans on the site of the modern City of London, in the late 40s AD, its population peaked at about 30,000 in the 2nd century. It then declined. In the medieval period the population again increased, reaching about 80,000 in 1300. This was almost halved by the Black Death in 1348-50 and it took some time for the population to grow once more. The late 1500s saw a huge increase, so that by 1600, the population was about 200,000. The four maps below show how the shape of London has changed from the late 17th to the 20th centuries, while retaining the River Thames as its focus. By 1800 London's population had reached about 1 million and by 1900 this had grown to around 6.5 million. Today there are about 8.6 million people living in London.

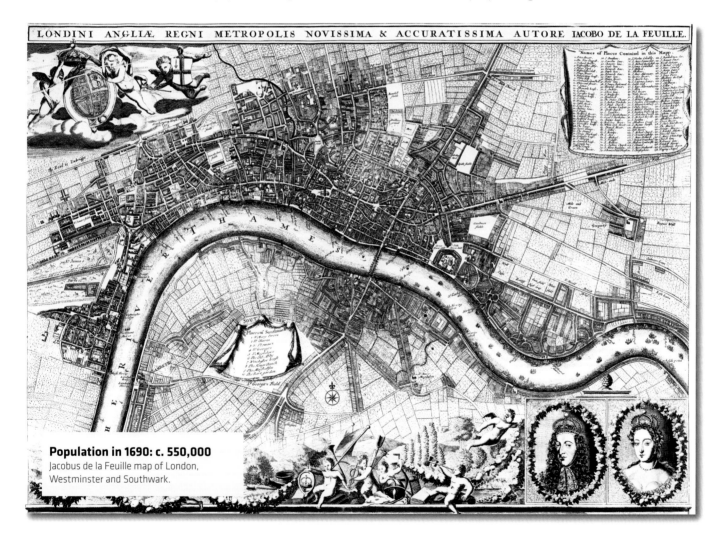

Population in 1690: c. 550,000
Jacobus de la Feuille map of London, Westminster and Southwark.

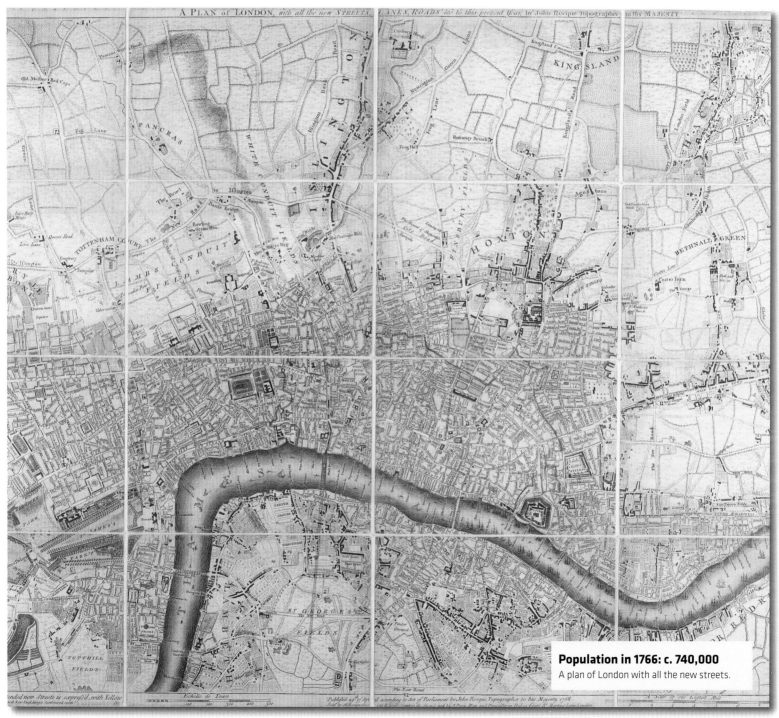

Population in 1766: c. 740,000

A plan of London with all the new streets.

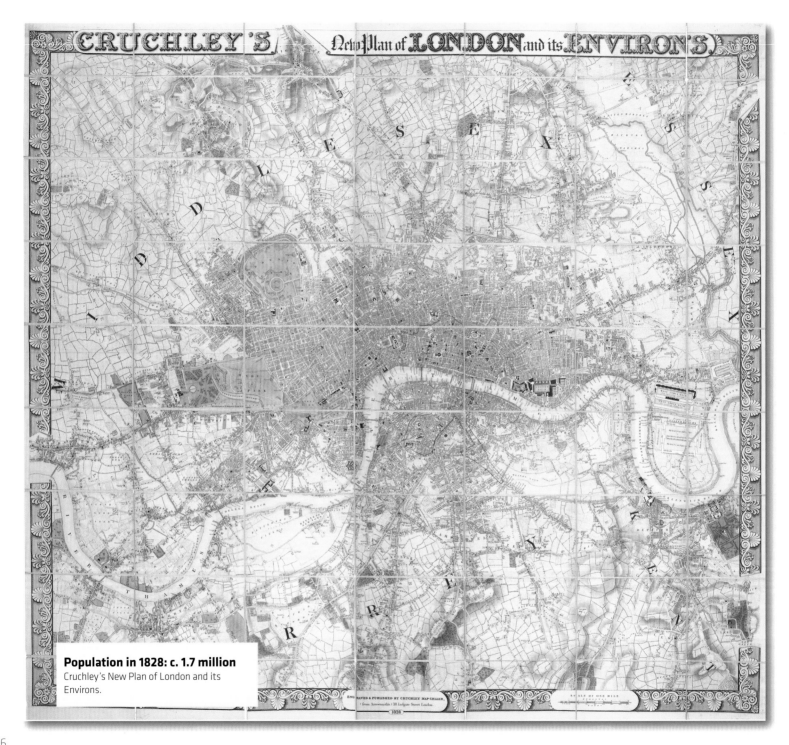

Population in 1828: c. 1.7 million
Cruchley's New Plan of London and its Environs.

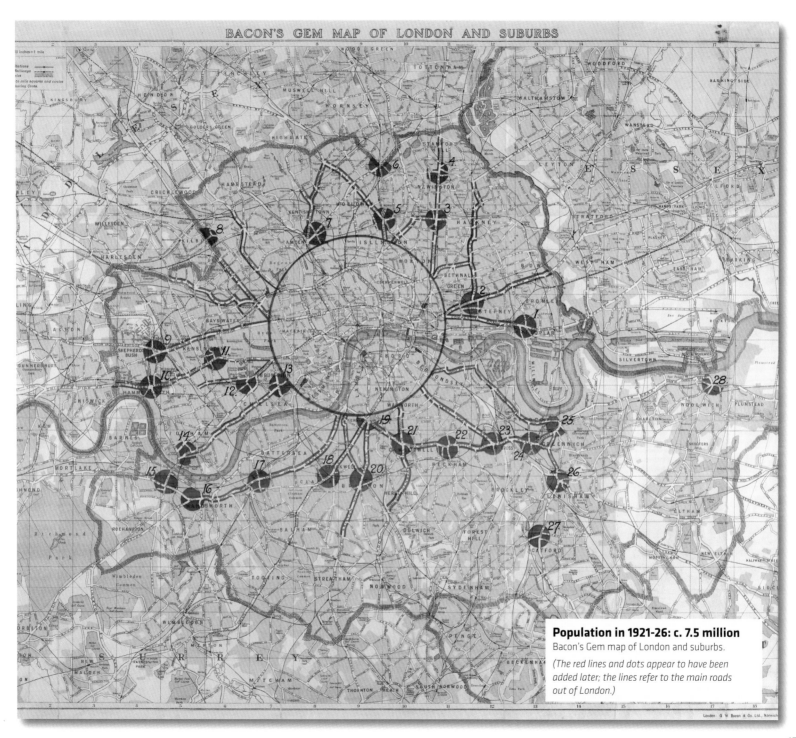

Population in 1921-26: c. 7.5 million
Bacon's Gem map of London and suburbs.

(The red lines and dots appear to have been added later; the lines refer to the main roads out of London.)

Archaeologists study people in the past by looking at the objects they used and the remains they left behind. There are many different types of archaeologist.

It was vital that the archaeological finds were preserved, analysed and recorded for future research, but the archaeologists had to be ready to get into sites at the right time, undertake their work and retreat to analyse their findings, before getting in the way of the programme of tunnelling and construction that was required to deliver a new railway for 2018.

A huge team of people worked on the archaeology programme, directed by Jay Carver, the Project Archaeologist at Crossrail. Jay undertook the design, planning and contract management of the full archaeology programme, seeing it through from its inception to the production of the final publications. Working closely with Jay, design archaeologists scheduled excavations to fit within the construction programme at each site. The team also worked closely with Historic England on all the planned archaeological works and historic building recording. The excavations were undertaken by four archaeology units: MOLA, Oxford Archaeology in partnership with Ramboll, and Wessex Archaeology.

Development partners involved in construction at Canary Wharf, Abbey Wood, Heathrow and other sites included Network Rail, Berkeley Homes, Canary Wharf Group and London Underground.

There are many different types of jobs in archaeology. Here are some of the archaeologists who worked on the Crossrail project:

Crossrail Project Archaeologist

Site Archaeologist

Human Osteologist

Geo-archaeologist

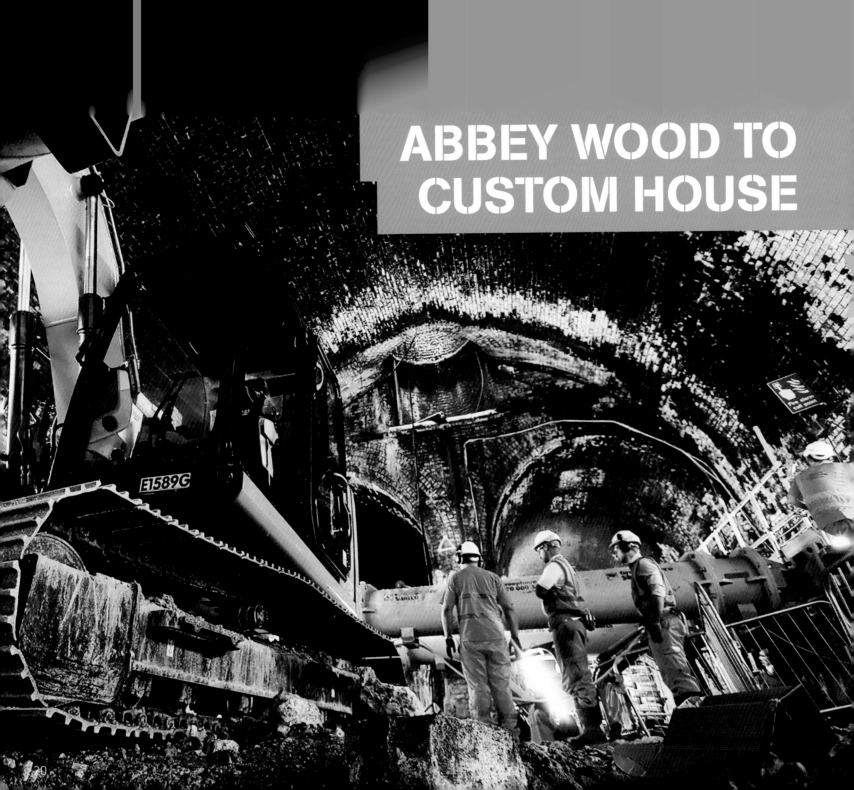

ABBEY WOOD TO CUSTOM HOUSE

The south-eastern section of the Crossrail project started at Abbey Wood, crossing the Thames via a new tunnel and resurfacing at North Woolwich. New portals were needed to integrate the existing surface railway with new tunnels in this area as the line travels under the Royal Docks, reusing the refurbished 19th century Connaught Tunnel.

Trial pits were investigated at Plumstead and North Woolwich where archaeological discoveries have increased our understanding of what the prehistoric landscape of south-east London looked like.

At the portal sites, archaeological excavations had to be undertaken after the new railway structures were built, to reduce the likelihood of additional ground movement and water influx caused by extensive digging.

"10,000 years ago the Thames valley was wide with clear-running freshwater channels and lakes."

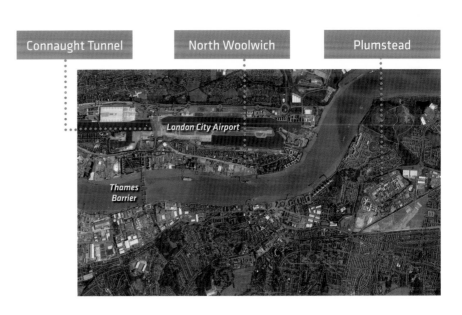

Connaught Tunnel   North Woolwich   Plumstead

London City Airport

Thames Barrier

Prehistoric south-east London

The Crossrail project has helped us to learn more about the prehistoric landscape of east and south-east London. Following the last Ice Age, from about 13,000 years ago the climate began to warm up and people and animals re-populated the Thames valley.

10,000 years ago the Thames valley was wide with clear-running freshwater channels and lakes. The river acted as a route through the densely wooded landscape, as well as a source of fresh water and food.

At North Woolwich archaeologists found evidence for evidence for a seasonal encampment in the lower Thames floodplain, dating to the later Mesolithic (c. 8,500 to 6,000 years ago). The site was located on what would have been an area of sandy, higher ground close to the river. Two scatters of struck flint were found, along with burnt flint and traces of hearths. The larger flint scatter indicates that someone had partly made a flint tool there, probably an axe or adze, leaving a scatter of flint waste. The activity can be dated by

GEOARCHAEOLOGY

Geoarchaeology is the study of landscapes and environments in the past, by looking at the types of soil and rocks that are found.

On the Crossrail project the geoarchaeologists worked closely with the Crossrail engineers studying the samples taken from deep below the ground surface.

This is a reconstruction of what the late Mesolithic tool-making site may have looked like. Most of the area was covered with dense woodland of lime, elm, oak, hazel and pine. The woodland was home to deer and other animals, which were hunted by the people living there.

Reconstruction drawing by Faith Vardy

23

The Crossrail site at North Woolwich was spread over a long narrow area. Archaeologists carried out careful research to decide where to excavate. One of these areas produced the Mesolithic flint waste, which you can see archaeologists excavating here.

About 8,000 years ago someone collected flint cobbles from the riverbed, sat down and began making an axe or adze. They struck off flakes with a hard stone hammer, roughly shaping the cobble. Flint axes, mounted onto wooden hafts, were used in carpentry or to cut down trees. These waste flakes are all that is left of that moment.

the presence of a small number of identifiable pieces, such as two microliths. This site is a rare survival. By their nature sites from this period are ephemeral – temporary campsites or toolmaking sites, such as this one, that were not in use for long. The material that is left behind, such as flint scatters or the traces of campfires, often does not survive.

At Plumstead, wooden stakes were found that had been shaped with a metal axe. These date to the Bronze Age, some 3,500 years ago, and were probably used in a walkway or track across the marshy wetlands, during a period of rising river levels.

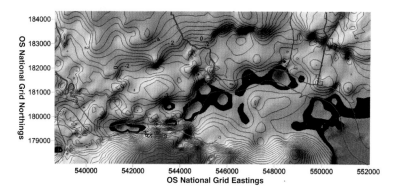

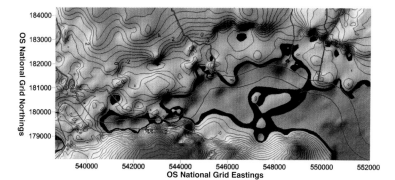

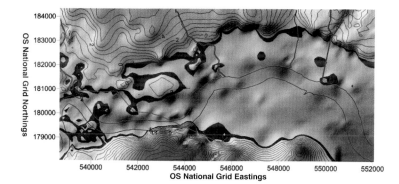

These three images show the changing water levels in the eastern Thames valley between about 10,000 and 5,000 years ago.

The line of the current River Thames is marked in dark blue. Soil samples taken from metres below ground level help archaeologists to build up a picture of what the landscape was like.

Archaeologists uncovered timber stakes, dating back 3,500 years. These are all that remain of a Bronze Age walkway or track.

Connaught Tunnel: the rebirth of a Victorian masterpiece

The Connaught Tunnel, originally called Silvertown Tunnel, was built in 1878-9 under the Royal Docks for the North London Railway. Closed since 2006, it was decided to reuse it for the Crossrail project.

The tunnel was expanded and refurbished over three years. This was difficult because it runs under a working dock which contains 13 million litres of water. The solution was to build two cofferdams – watertight enclosures – directly above the tunnel. Each cofferdam was the size of a football pitch. The water was drained so that the work could be carried out. Specialist divers placed a one metre thick, reinforced concrete slab on the floor of the dock to protect the tunnel's roof. The draining and refilling of the dock took three months.

Work involved cleaning away 135 years' worth of dirt and soot. Added complications included avoiding shows at the adjacent ExCeL centre and arranging for the rescue of fish caught in the cofferdams. One of the historic buildings associated with the tunnel was deconstructed for use elsewhere.

The existing tunnels were too narrow for the modern trains and so had to be expanded and relined.

(Left) The dock beneath which the tunnel runs had to be drained of its water and then refilled.

Laying the new rail track through the refurbished Connaught Tunnel.

CANNING TOWN TO CANARY WHARF

North of Victoria Dock, near Canning Town, the line plunges underground again to begin its journey under central London. A vast shaft was excavated at the Limmo Peninsula for the giant tunnelling machinery to be lowered into.

Here, before the tunnelling could begin, hundreds of tonnes of soil were removed to allow archaeologists to investigate one of the great industrial sites of London. The 21-strong archaeology team studied the Thames Iron Works, increasing our knowledge of London's 19th century shipbuilding industry.

"Archaeologists found the remains of buildings associated both with shipbuilding and the iron works, as well as parts of the slipways used for launching ships."

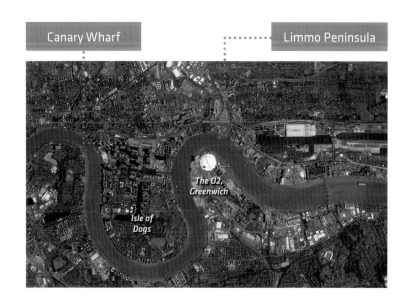

Canary Wharf

Limmo Peninsula

The O2, Greenwich

Isle of Dogs

The Thames Iron Works

The Thames Iron Works and Shipbuilding Company (1837-1912) was founded at a time when most ships were built from wood. It was at the forefront of the innovation to use iron to build ships.

Despite changes in ownership and fluctuations in its fortunes, the company played a major role in the history of British iron shipbuilding. It produced ships for the Royal Navy (including HMS Warrior and HMS Thunderer) and many foreign navies, as well as private yachts for Queen Victoria and the Pope. It also undertook civil engineering projects, such as Blackfriars railway bridge and Hammersmith suspension bridge in London and the Kotri bridge in Pakistan. The works closed in 1912.

Archaeologists found the remains of buildings associated with both shipbuilding and the iron works, as well as parts of the slipways used for launching ships. Objects found included part of a massive iron chain and many structural items, such as bricks. A halfpenny coin was found near one of the slipways. The coin dates to 1862, the year the slipway was built.

Many of the bricks found were firebricks, which were used to line the flues of the ironworks' furnaces. A number had names or initials stamped on their faces. Two of the most common names were 'POTTER' and 'COWEN'. The 'POTTER' bricks were made in Scotland and date to the 1860s-1880s, whilst the 'COWEN' bricks were produced at Blaydon-on-Tyne, Newcastle between c. 1823 and 1904. One brick, stamped 'M.T & Co', is more unusual and is the first example known from London. It is not known where these bricks were made. Bricks with the same mark have been found in California, including at Alcatraz prison.

Archaeologists record the exposed timbers of the south slipway.

LONGEST TUNNEL

The tunnel running from the Limmo peninsula to Farringdon was the longest section of tunnel to be bored on the project. It is 8.3 kilometres long and took three years to build.

When Cleopatra's Needle was brought from Egypt to London in 1877, the company built the iron framework and cylinder ship used to transport it. The ship and its ancient-Egyptian cargo were nearly lost in a storm in the Bay of Biscay. The enormous stone obelisk was presented to Britain in 1819 by the ruler of Egypt in commemoration of Lord Nelson's victory at the Battle of the Nile and Sir Ralph Abercromby's at the Battle of Alexandria in 1801. The obelisk remained in Egypt until 1877 when Sir William Erasamus Wilson sponsored its transportation to London.

Evidence of much earlier Thames ships was also found. This is part of the starboard side of a small barge or fishing vessel made between 1223 and 1290. It is clinker-built with overlapping oak boards and iron rivets.

Some of the buildings uncovered included the floor of the engineers' shop, in the foreground, the engine house, behind, and the pipe shop to the left of the picture.

This large iron chain was found near the south slipway and may have been used to secure the ships there or to help slow them down during launching.

0mm   210mm   420mm

HMS Warrior

The ironclad warship, HMS Warrior, was built by the company and can still be seen today. When launched in 1860 she was the largest and fastest warship in existence. In places her hull was two feet thick, combining iron plates and teak. Today she is berthed at Portsmouth and is open to the public.

The launch of HMS Albion at the Thames Iron Works in 1898 was one of the worst ever peacetime tragedies on the Thames. Some 30,000 people had crowded onto the shore to watch. As the ship launched the backwash drowned 38 people, including children. A memorial to those lost in the disaster can be found in the East London Cemetery.

West Ham United Football Club was set up in 1895 for the workers at the Thames Iron Works and Shipbuilding Company. The club's crest includes two crossed hammers. Hammers like this were used by riveters at the company. Each hammer is marked TIW for Thames Iron Works. The club is popularly known as the 'Hammers' or the 'Irons'.

Mammoths at Canary Wharf

The new Canary Wharf station with its retail and leisure development above, was built in the dock on the north of the Canary Wharf estate. The dock was drained to allow for construction and samples to be taken from deep under Canary Wharf. These produced a fragment of amber and part of a woolly mammoth's jaw bone. The amber was found in the middle of a bore sample that was extracted 15 metres below the current dock bed at Canary Wharf. Given the site had been deemed unlikely to yield archaeological finds and that the bore sample was only 10cm in diameter, it was an accidental but very lucky discovery. As was the mammoth jaw fragment, which was spotted by a sharp eyed construction worker as the dock was drained.

The amber is estimated to be 55 million years old and is the oldest amber to have been found in London. Amber is

Amber found at Cannary Wharf is estimated to be 55 million years old

fossilised tree resin and it is very rare to find it in the London area. It is currently being analysed at the Natural History Museum because of its importance. The amber may hold information about what the landscape and environment of this area was like at the time.

The mammoth bone is also being analysed at the Natural History Museum. It comes from the jaw of a woolly mammoth which would have roamed the Thames valley some time between 100,000 and 12,000 years ago, during the last Ice Age. The remains of woolly mammoths have been found at a number of sites around London. The complete skull of an earlier type of mammoth, a 200,000 year old steppe mammoth, was discovered in Ilford in 1864. Mammoths became extinct in Western Europe around 12,000 years ago, when the climate began to get warmer.

Part of the jaw bone of a woolly mammoth. It comes from a young individual. Fully-grown male woolly mammoths were about 3.2 metres high at the shoulder and females about 2.8 metres high.

SHENFIELD TO PUDDING MILL LANE

This section of the Elizabeth line will link central London to Shenfield in Essex. It partially uses existing rail lines, but to connect these to the rest of the route a tunnel running 2.7 kilometres was bored from Pudding Mill Lane to Stepney Green, creating a new link between Stratford and Whitechapel.

A site in the Pudding Mill Lane area was identified as potentially of interest and archaeologists worked to uncover finds prior to the ongoing construction of the route. The work yielded new information about how the River Lea was used and managed in the past.

"In medieval times meadows by the river Lea were used for grazing animals and the river itself for flour mills and fishing."

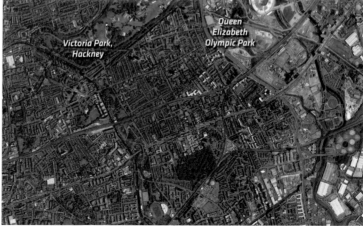

Pudding Mill Lane

Victoria Park, Hackney

Queen Elizabeth Olympic Park

Pudding Mill Lane: industries on the River Lea

Pudding Mill Lane, adjacent to the River Lea, is where the north-eastern section tunnels underground. The river, which runs from Hertfordshire to the north, down into the Thames in east London, has had a variety of uses.

In medieval times its meadows were used for grazing animals and the river itself for flour mills and fishing. The name Pudding Mill is thought to derive from a nickname for one of these early mills which resembled an upturned pudding. Fragmentary wooden structures that were found may be the remains of fish weirs. They have been dated to between the late 13th to early 17th centuries and were likely to have been placed in the river to trap fish.

(Right) Archaeologists excavate the late 13th to early 17th century timber structures on the River Lea

(Below) Scene on the River Lea, 1788

By the 19th century the industries on the Lea were far more noxious and included heavy chemical works. They employed many people and were accompanied by increased housing, shops and places of entertainment, such as public houses. A pewter measure and complete glass bottle probably relate to the latter. The measure holds a quart (a quarter of a gallon or two pints) and was made between 1850 and 1880. It is inscribed 'G. Kent / Albion / Old Ford', referring to the Albion public house on Old Ford Road. Its spout is missing. The bottle is stamped 'UFFINDELL / 3 CUPS / 5 BOW HIGH ST'. In the 1856 Post Office directory, The Three Cups public house was owned by William Uffindell and was located at 5 Bow High St.

Glass bottle and pewter measure, late 1800s

Bow Locks, River Lea today

STEPNEY GREEN

Stepney Green is where the south-eastern and north-eastern section of the Elizabeth line join to run west.

A number of sites were excavated here in advance of the construction of an access shaft and huge underground cavern where trains will cross over to either the Abbey Wood or Stratford routes when the railway opens.

These sites lay to the west of the church of St Dunstan and All Saints, Stepney and included part of Stepney City Farm.

A significant dig, the 35-strong team studied the sites and recovered hundreds of objects, painting a fascinating story of the area's changing fortunes over 500 years.

"In the 1860s cholera killed more residents in Stepney than any other London borough. This led to the belated extension of mains sewers to the East End."

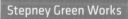

Stepney Green Works

Mile End Stadium

Moated manor house to Victorian terrace

Excavations uncovered the remains of a 15th century moated manor house. King John's Court or Palace was home to the wealthy Fenne family. Rubbish thrown into the moat gives an insight into the lives of those who lived in the manor house. Fragments of expensive Venetian glass were found, while a dress pin and a decoratively slashed shoe hint at what the inhabitants wore. The moat also produced evidence of what they ate, including charred wheat and pulses, such as peas.

From the early 17th century the manor house became known as Worcester House after its owner the Marquis of Worcester. A brick cesspit (a pit, usually in the backyard, for toilet waste) produced pottery dating to c. 1570-1610, as well as fragments of English glass vessels. Most of the pottery was for the storage, preparation or serving of food. It was largely made around London, or in Surrey and Hampshire, but some was also imported from the Netherlands, Germany and Spain.

(Below) In Victorian times most houses did not have indoor toilets. So people kept a chamber pot in their bedroom to go to the toilet in at night. In the morning they would throw the contents into a hole in their back yard called a cesspit. Sometimes chamber pots had funny pictures and rhymes on them, such as this one that was made in Sunderland. The motto on the inside reads: 'Oh what I see / I will not tell'.

(Above) This small ceramic vessel was probably made in Spain after about 1500. It has thick walls and may have been used to hold mercury, which was used in medicine at this time. It may have belonged to the physician, Richard Mead, who lived here from 1696 to 1719.

During the English Civil War, the manor house was confiscated and passed to Maurice Thompson, a merchant, Puritan and parliamentarian. Under his patronage the Stepney Meeting of Religious Non-Conformists was founded in 1644. Its first pastor was William Greenhill, a radical cleric, under whose guidance it flourished as a safe haven for early Protestant non-conformists. In the 1660s, the manor house and grounds were divided, with the then pastor of the Stepney Meeting, Matthew Meade, living in part of the house. He built a separate meeting house in the grounds. A college, church and school were later added, the latter two surviving until they were damaged by bombing in World War II. The college was demolished in the 19th century and the site used for terraced housing.

In the early 19th century the remaining parts of Worcester House were demolished and a road, Garden Street, and houses were built. Some of the houses had wells, which were excavated by the archaeologists and produced pottery and other items, including a nutcracker and brooch. They also produced the remains of exotic spices such as black pepper and allspice.

In the 1860s cholera killed more residents in Stepney than any other London borough. This led to the belated extension of mains sewers to the East End. The cesspits in the backyards of the houses on Garden Street were abandoned. They were filled in with rubbish, including many pots and other items.

Reconstruction of Worcester House and estate in the late 15th to 16th century. The house had a roughly square plan and was surrounded by a moat.

Reconstruction drawing by Faith Vardy

BAPTIST COLLEGE, STEPNEY.

This wooden ball was excavated from the moat of the Tudor manor house. It may have been used as a 'jack' in a game of bowls or skittles. Ball games were very popular with the wealthy at this time. King Henry VIII loved bowls but banned poor people from playing it.

(Above) The Baptist College occupied the Stepney Green Road frontage of Worcester House between 1810 and 1855. The section in the middle with the tower is the remains of the gatehouse of the Tudor manor house. This illustration from around 1840 is by R Cartwright.

Local community involvement was an important part of the Crossrail project.
(Right) It included a community excavation with local school children. Another was an oral history project, recording local people's memories of World War II.

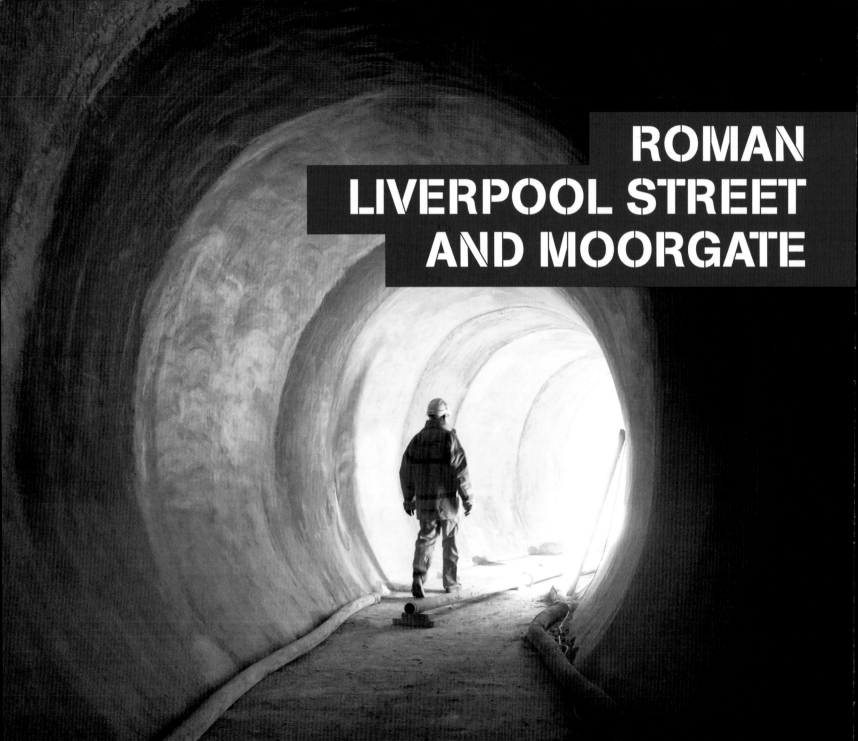

ROMAN
LIVERPOOL STREET
AND MOORGATE

A series of archaeological excavations were carried out at Finsbury Circus, during the construction of an access shaft, and at Moorgate and Broadgate where the two new ticket halls for Liverpool Street station were being built.

A part of London inhabited since Roman times, early research pointed to this being one of the richest sources of archaeology on the route. The largest dig was to the south of the old Broad Street station, west of Liverpool Street station

Unusually on the project, here the entire footprint of the new ticket hall was excavated. One of the deepest and most complex of digs on the Crossrail project this site turned out to be the most archaeologically rich. Eighty archaeologists worked on the site intermittently over a five year period and retrieved thousands of objects, many of them Roman.

No other site better illustrates the layers of history beneath the streets of London where different depths of excavation revealed Roman, medieval and Victorian artefacts.

"To the south of the road eight burials were found. Three of these were decapitations, one with the head placed between the legs."

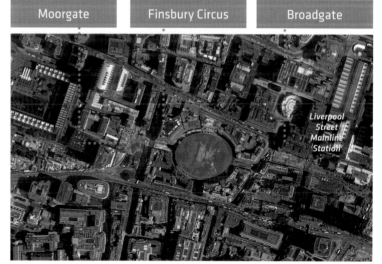

| Moorgate | Finsbury Circus | Broadgate |

The Roman Walbrook river

In Roman times this part of London, just north of the City wall, was dominated by the Walbrook river which flowed south into the Thames.

The large excavation at Liverpool Street lay on the eastern bank of the Walbrook. There was little activity here until AD 120 when a road was built across the site to the north and a platform was built on the riverbank using two wooden gates. The wood for the gates was identified by dendrochronology as having been cut between AD 110 and 134.

The road's surface survived so well in places that wheel ruts could be seen. Towards the end of the Roman period, the ground became increasingly marshy. There are a number of reasons why this happened. In the late 2nd and early 3rd century the city wall was built around the settlement and the river was diverted beneath it. This, however, appears not to have been very successful and the construction of the wall is frequently seen as a cause of the subsequent development of the marsh. In addition, by this time the population of Londinium was in decline and the levels of water management that had been in evidence earlier disappeared. Added to this, climate change in the later Roman period saw increased rainfall. All of these factors led to the development of a marsh which was to last into the medieval period.

Animals moved along the Roman road, carrying people and goods, and they were probably also kept nearby. Large numbers of horse bones and horse-related objects found here, indicate that this may have been an area where horses were kept.

The Roman wooden gates during excavation.

DENDROCHRONOLOGY

Dendrochronology is a way of finding out how old a tree is. If you saw through a tree trunk you can see rings in the wood. Each year a tree grows a new ring so that by counting the rings it is possible to work out how old the tree is. We can do the same for large wooden items, such as the gates found at this site.

53

Seventeen hipposandals (temporary iron horseshoes) were found on or near the Roman road, as well as terrets (horse harness rings) and ox goads for prodding animals. The remains of at least five horses were recovered from deposits associated with the road and ditch. Roman horses were the size of a modern pony, but three of those found were quite large and may have been cavalry horses. Some of the bones showed knife marks indicating the flesh had been removed. The Romans did not eat horse meat and so this is likely to have been removed for dog food.

(Right) Archaeologists excavate and record the Roman road.

A selection of the hipposandals from the archaeological excavations.

This very rare bronze medallion, of Emperor Phillip I (Arabicus), was found during the excavations at Liverpool Street. It was issued to mark the New Year celebrations in AD 245 and is only the second example ever found. It would have been presented by the emperor to important government or military officials.

Roman Coins

Apart from the medallion, 105 Roman coins were recovered from the excavation at Liverpool Street. The majority are copper alloy, with seven in silver and a small number silver-plated. The earliest coins found date to around the time of the conquest of Britain in AD 43 and are of the Emperor Claudius I (AD 43-54). The latest coins belong to the 4th century, dating to AD 330 to 348.

If a coin is in good condition it is possible to identify not only who the emperor is and therefore what date it is but also where it was minted. Most early Roman coins were minted in Rome but from the 3rd century on other mints became common too. There was a mint in Londinium from about AD 286 until AD 326. The Roman coins from Liverpool Street come from as far away as Antioch (in modern Turkey), from Rome and from the London mint.

A selection of the coins are pictured (right). They feature, clockwise from top right: Hadrian AD119-121, Licinius AD 316, Carausius AD 287-293 (minted in London), Gallienus AD 257, Septimus Severus AD 201, and in the centre Carausius AD 287-293. These include three with a connection to Britain.

Hadrian was emperor from AD 117 to 138. He was the only emperor to travel widely through his empire, including a visit to Britain in AD 122. The most lasting result of this visit was the construction of Hadrian's Wall in the north of England.

Septimus Severus ruled from AD 198 to 211. He came from Libya in North Africa. His accession brought to an end a period of civil war in the Empire. From 209 he led a campaign to conquer Scotland, but died in York in 211.

Carausius was a military commander in the Roman navy. In 286/7 he declared himself emperor of Britain and northern Gaul and established a coin mint in London. He was assassinated after ruling his breakaway empire for seven years.

Many everyday Roman items were found, from pots and tools to brooches and bracelets. Most of these were found in the soil that was dumped over the road or elsewhere on the site. It is likely that some of these objects came from burials in the area that were later disturbed. Many pieces of jewellery and other small personal items were found, including a small phallic-shaped belt mount made of copper-alloy. Mounts and pendants in the form of a penis were common in Roman life and were thought to bring luck to the wearer.

An iron shackle was found, which was probably used on a prisoner or slave in Roman London. There is written evidence from writing tablets for slaves living in London but we know little of what their lives were like in detail or of how they were treated.

The small phallic belt mount, which was probably worn as a symbol of good luck.

A number of complete or near complete pots were found, particularly in the ditch. It is unusual to find so many complete pots and it is likely that most came from burials or cremations that were disturbed by later activity. Most were made in or near to London, in particular at the pottery kilns in Highgate Wood in north London.

ARCHAEOBOTANY

To find out what the vegetation and environment of a place was like in the past, archaeobotanists look at samples of soil. They study the traces of plants in the soil. On this site they found the remains of wetland plants, including those that grow in shallow water or close to marshy or muddy places.

X7886

The iron ring, shown in the X-ray to the left, was very corroded when found and the X-ray helped in identifying its original form. It was found on the right wrist of an adult male skeleton. Unfortunately the left arm had been disturbed, probably when a sewer was constructed in the 19th century, and so it was not possible to say if there had been an accompanying ring on the left wrist. The ring is large enough to fit over a human hand but too heavy to have been a comfortable adornment in life. It was welded shut and so could not have functioned as a conventional shackle. Its purpose is not known but it may have been placed on the arm symbolically, as part of the burial ritual, perhaps to represent a shackle or as a form of punishment. Alternatively it may have been placed in some sort of recognition of the person it was buried with, perhaps denoting them as a slave. Burials with iron rings have been found before but are not common and so it may not necessarily be representative of a slave, a class that would have been common in Roman London.

The Roman cemetery

A cemetery lay in this area to the north east of the Roman settlement. During the Roman period, some of the burials appear to have been disturbed by activity, such as dumping, reclamation and work on the road.

To the south of the road eight burials were found. Three of these were decapitations, one with the head placed between the legs. Analysis of the bones indicated that the heads were removed with sharp bladed weapons. It is uncertain whether the heads were removed through execution, perhaps of prisoners, or after death, perhaps as a burial ritual. Decapitated burials are known from elsewhere in London and the rest of Britain. It is interesting that more examples of decapitated burials have been found in Britain than anywhere else in the Roman Empire and so it may be that it is a continuation of a pre-Roman burial tradition.

To the west of these burials a charnel pit was found, where human remains had been gathered together for re-burial, perhaps indicating a cleaning up of part of the cemetery that had been disturbed. A cremation urn was found to the west of the site. It was recovered from the ceiling of a sewer tunnel at the very west of the site. It was made at kilns in Brockley Hill in north west London and was probably originally buried with a ceramic lid. The vessel contained the remains of a single individual, almost certainly an adult.

(Left) The Brockley Hill urn and a computed tomography (CT) scan of it (above) showing its contents.

CT scan by Olivia Egan, CT Superintendent Radiographer, Chelsea and Westminster Hospital

The mystery of the Walbrook skulls

During the excavation more than 50 human skulls along with a smaller number of other human bones were recovered from Roman deposits. These add to about 300 skulls that have been found in and around the upper Walbrook valley over the last 200 years. There has been much debate about why these disarticulated human remains appear in this area.

The majority of the skulls at the Liverpool Street site are from adult males and were found in two different types of locations. Twenty-one skulls were found in the earliest roadside ditch, which was dug in the mid-2nd century AD. They may have been deliberately placed there. But where did they come from?

A further 35 skulls were recovered from gravel which was dumped on the eastern bank of the Walbrook, towards the end of the 2nd century, a possible attempt at raising the ground level to stabilise the bank. Radiocarbon dating of these skulls indicates they come from a number of different dates within the Roman period. Some showed signs of damage from the gravel – one has pebbles lodged in its eye socket - while others had water lines as if they had been lying in standing water. It is not known where they originated from.

Archaeology discovers information but not always the explanation and it is likely that the skulls and other human remains in the Walbrook are there due to a combination of factors.

Q & A

Were only skulls found?

No, although fewer in number, other human bones have also been found.

Are the skulls complete?

No. The neck or cervical vertebrae and the lower jaws (mandibles) are missing. These are the bones that would show if they had been beheaded. Their presence would indicate that these were intact heads rather than detached skulls.

Could the skulls come from the Boudican revolt in AD60/61?

No, dating of the skulls and archaeological evidence indicates they are later than this.

Could the skulls be evidence for another uprising in Roman London?

Carvings on Trajan's column in Rome show defeated troops from Dacia being decapitated by the Roman army. Could these skulls be evidence of the aftermath of a rebellion in 2nd century London? This would seem unlikely since the skulls are from people who died at different times.

Could some of the skulls have been washed out of a cemetery by flooding of the Walbrook?

This might explain why many of the skulls ended up in this area, which is surrounded by Roman burial grounds.

Are the skulls evidence for the continuation of a pre-Roman head cult?

Head cults, where heads are displayed as war trophies or part of a ritual, are known from the pre-Roman Iron Age but there is no evidence for them in Roman London. It is possible that skulls washed out of graves may have been deliberately collected and carefully reburied in pits and ditches.

The McNicholas Miners

Working on busy construction sites requires a close working relationship between archaeologists and building contractors. At the Liverpool Street site, for health and safety reasons, only trained miners could enter one of the tunnels which had to be hand-excavated by them..

The McNicholas miners worked closely with archaeologists so that the archaeology could be recorded. The miners took photographs every metre along the tunnel, so that archaeologists could see what they were finding and record it. The miners also recovered a number of human skulls and a complete cremation urn with its contents. The latter was caught by miner Keith Hancock (below) when it fell from the tunnel's ceiling.

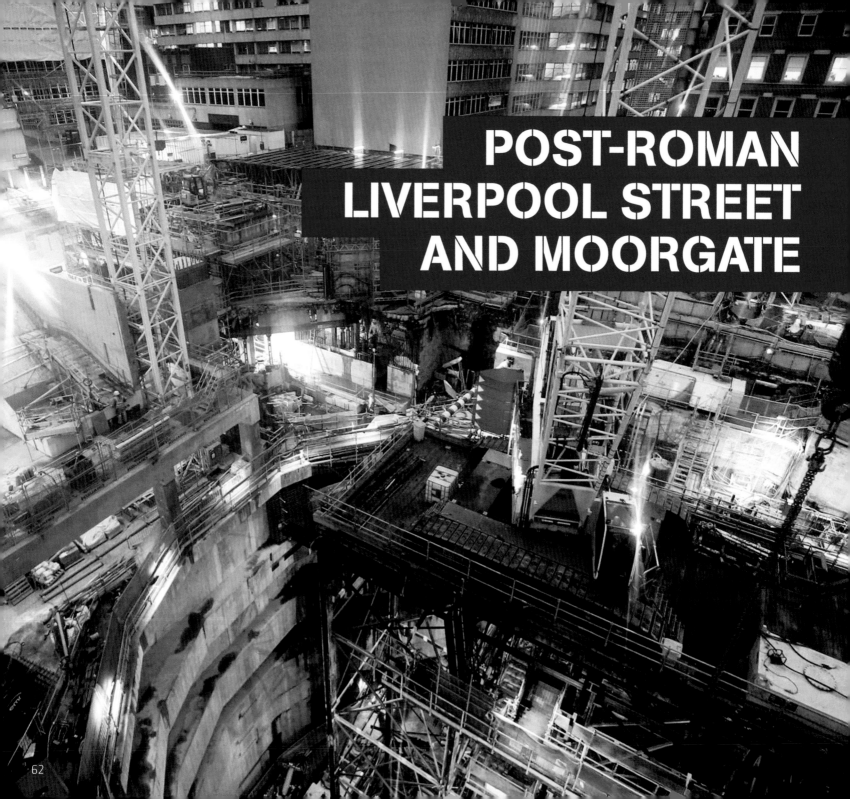

POST-ROMAN LIVERPOOL STREET AND MOORGATE

Excavations of the post-Roman layers at Liverpool Street uncovered marshy areas adjacent to the Walbrook. The land was consolidated and from 1569 to 1772 was part of the New Churchyard. In the 19th century much of it was taken over by the development of the railways.

"Among these was a mass grave containing 42 individuals, but which may have originally held more than 100. It is thought to have been dug during one of the plague outbreaks in the late 16th or early 17th century."

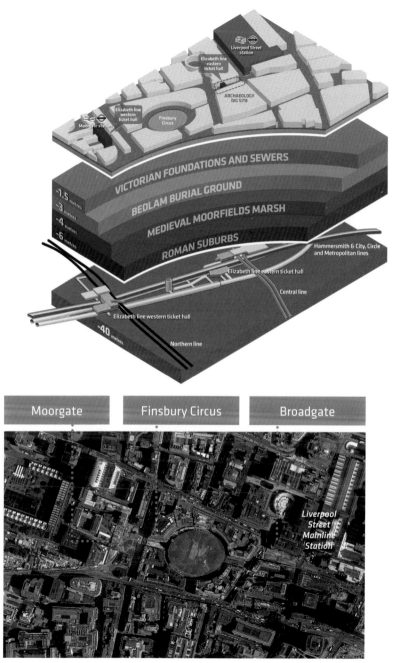

The Moorfields Marsh

Due to the marshy nature of the land, the area to the north of the City wall became known as Moorfields. Throughout the medieval period efforts were made to manage the water flow.

The Walbrook was re-named the 'Deep Ditch' and timber revetments (retaining walls) were built. Remains of these were found during the excavations.

An additional gate in the wall, Moorgate, was built in the 15th century but development remained largely along the road that ran north out of the City. In the 16th century the 'Deep Ditch' was re-cut to the east of the original Walbrook. By the mid- to late 16th century it had become an open sewer and rubbish dump. The nature of the area changed again with the establishment of the 'New Churchyard' in 1569.

Many items were recovered from the marshy ground and in particular from the 'Deep Ditch'. They date to the 15th and 16th centuries. The earliest objects are three animal bone ice skates. William FitzStephen, writing in the late 12th century, described how young men would tie animal bones to their feet and skate on the frozen marsh at Moorfields in winter.

The damp conditions also preserved leather items, including shoes dating to the 15th to 16th centuries. Many small metal dress accessories were found that would have been used for fastening clothing, such as pins, a buckle and small hooked tags. Lace-chapes are small pieces of sheet metal that re-enforced the ends of laces and ribbons used to tie clothing. A small decorative mount depicts two men on horseback.

Pilgrim souvenirs were another form of dress accessory. These small decorative objects, often badges and usually made of lead alloy, were brought back from religious pilgrimages between the late 12th and early 16th centuries. Medieval pilgrims travelled widely, to Compostela in Spain or even to Rome. The souvenirs they brought home with them showed where they had been and the shrines they had visited. More importantly, however, these objects were thought to be imbued with miraculous healing

Two of the bone ice skates (left) and one of the leather shoes (above) found during the excavations.

The Moorfields area is seen right, in a detail from the Copperplate map of 1553-59. It shows it as a largely open area used for cloth processing and archery practice among other activities.

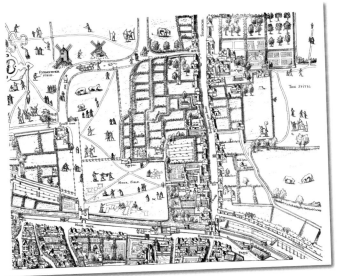

65

powers. The badges and souvenirs found on this site illustrate the range of shrines that could be visited. One of the badges may represent St Martin of Tours in France, an example of one of the many continental shrines that were visited by Londoners. But other shrines, much more local to London, were popular too and offered the less well-off pilgrim a more realistic option for travel. The excavation produced a number of badges, all of the same design, which are thought to be of Our Lady of Willesden. Two small mounts in copper-alloy are slightly later in date, probably 15th to 16th century. They are of the Annunciation and of St George and the Dragon. The Annunciation badge may be associated with the shrine to the Virgin Mary at Walsingham in Norfolk, while the St George and the Dragon example is probably associated with the Chapel of St George at Windsor. Again these are examples of more accessible shrines for the citizens of London.

The many thimbles that were found show that home-based industries including sewing and tailoring were common. Pinners' bones, which were used by pin-makers to file the points on lengths of wire when making them into pins, were also found. Small iron tenterhooks were used in the processing and drying of cloth. Coins and jettons, used for accounting, were common in medieval and Tudor London. In particular many Nuremberg jettons dating from the late 15th to mid 16th century were found, along with one from Tournai and two 'Venus pennies' from the Low Countries. Coins included a penny of Edward IV (1471-83) and a silver half-penny of Henry VII or VIII. The most

(Left) From top to bottom: a copper-alloy mount depicting the Annunciation and probably from Walsingham in Norfolk; a copper-alloy mount of St George and the Dragon, probably from Windsor; and one of the lead-alloy badges probably from Willesden, depicting the Virgin Mary holding the Christ child in a crescent moon.

unusual coin is a gold half ducat of Leonardo Loredan, the Doge of Venice, dating to 1501-21. It had been pierced perhaps to be worn as a necklace or attached to clothing as a sequin.

Other items recovered included household items such as ceramic vessels and implements, as well as tools and other items used in manufacturing. They date to between the 15th and 16th centuries. Pottery includes imported wares from the Netherlands, Beauvais in France, and Germany. Locally produced vessels were also found, including chafing dishes for warming food. Food waste included grape seeds, plum stones, and pieces of walnut and hazelnut, as well as animal, fish and bird bones. The latter includes a single bone belonging to the then newly discovered species, the North American turkey.

(Above) Unusual imported ceramic pots were also found. This is part of a basil pot or plant pot, made by Moorish potters near Valencia in the early 15th century. It was found on the excavation at Moorgate and is thought to be the first time this type of vessel has been found on an archaeological site in Britain.

(Left) An archaeologist excavates a leather shoe from the damp, marsh deposits.

The New Churchyard

The New Churchyard was the first of the early modern non-parochial City burial grounds. It was established on land that had been part of the priory of St Mary Bethlehem and so became known as the Bethlehem Churchyard or the Old Bethlehem Burying Ground. This was often abbreviated to Bethlem or Bedlam. The churchyard remained in use for 170 years and closed in 1739.

In the 1860s, when Broad Street station and accompanying railway tracks were being built, the churchyard was disturbed and human skeletons were found and removed. Amongst these were the remains of the pet cat of the antiquarian, Charles Roach Smith. Some years previously Roach Smith, a businessman who had a keen interest in Roman antiquities and was a founder of the British Archaeological Association, had his servant bury the cat in land across the road from where he lived at 5 Liverpool Street. The servant had reported that when burying the cat he had also come across human bones. Roach Smith recorded the re-discovery of the cat:

'A few years later the cat's coffin and epitaph were bought before the directors of the North London and Great Eastern Railway as a very puzzling discovery!'

Interestingly the Crossrail offices for this part of the project were located on the site of 5 Liverpool Street!

The Crossrail excavations, in the new ticket hall site, lay within the south-western part of the burial ground and over 3,300 burials were uncovered. Amongst these was a mass

Archaeologists excavate some of the 3,300 burials discovered at the Liverpool Street site. The information about each skeleton is recorded onto special recording sheets.

grave containing 42 individuals, but which may have originally held more than 100. It is thought to have been dug during one of the plague outbreaks in the late 16th or 17th century. The Great Plague of 1665 is the most famous outbreak. It killed 100,000 people in London, almost a quarter of the population.

A project to record the burial registers for the New Churchyard was undertaken with volunteer helpers and the assistance of the London Metropolitan Archives. Using the original registers they recorded the names and other details of those who had died and been buried there. This information included details of the cause of death and age of the deceased. The resulting database includes over 5,000 records and is available via the Crossrail website (www.crossrail.co.uk).

Ten stone grave markers were found at the site. One is for Mary Godfree (right), who died on 2 September 1665, a victim of the Great Plague.

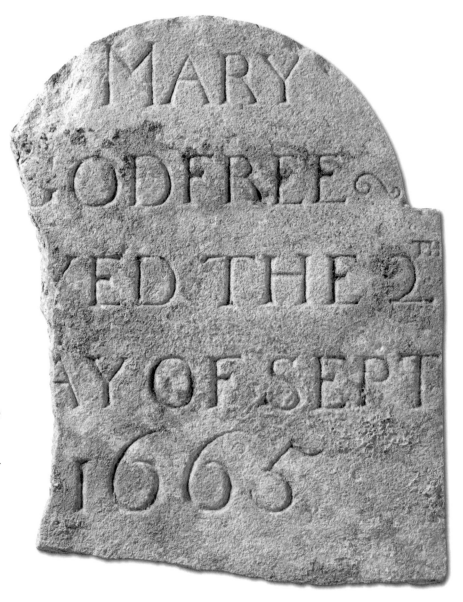

From documentary sources it is known that the New Churchyard was used as an emergency burial ground during plague epidemics. The most famous of these epidemics is the Great Plague of 1665, which killed almost a quarter of London's population.

The Great Plague was the last major outbreak of what is called the Second Plague Pandemic. This was a period of history, from 1347/8 through to the 18th century, which saw periodic outbreaks of plague in Europe. The Great Plague reached a peak in the summer of 1665, when the king, court and whoever could afford to, left London to try and escape it. The Bills of Mortality in London for 1665 record that about 70% of deaths that year were due to the plague.

It had long been assumed that the New Churchyard had been used as an emergency burial ground during major plague epidemics. The Crossrail excavations have now confirmed this. Five of the individuals from the mass grave have tested positive for the plague pathogen. This is the first ever identification of plague DNA from 16th-17th century Britain.

A number of objects were found that had been deliberately placed in burials. A set of glass and stone beads were found with the skeleton of an infant.

A London delftware plate depicts a well-known design, 'Chinaman among grasses' and dates to 1670-90. It had been placed in the coffin, face down, over the stomach area of the skeleton. A pewter plate was also found in a similar position in another burial.

The beads (above), shown here on a modern string, were found scattered around the neck of a one year old child. The beads are amber, white amber, carnelian, glass and bone.

The London-made delftware plate (right) was found face down on the stomach of an adult woman (above). It may have contained salt, thought to be both a preservative and a protection against the devil.

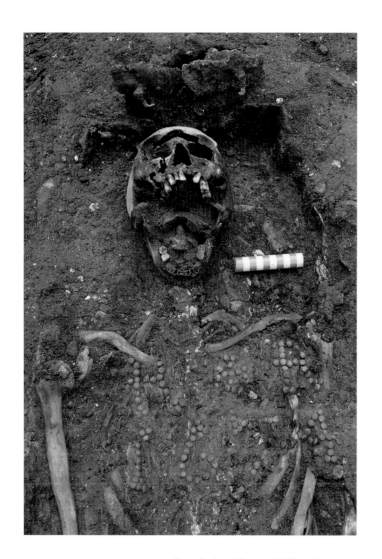

From the late 17th to mid-18th century decorated coffin lids were popular. Eleven were found with biographical details (usually initials and date of death). The earliest is shown on the left: 'RR 1674'. The example on the right reads 'PW 1676'.

Scientific analysis of human remains

The study of infectious diseases, such as the Great Plague, is difficult in skeletal assemblages due to their acute nature which leaves no trace on the bones. However, recent developments in the analysis of ancient DNA (aDNA) have meant that it is now possible to test for and identify diseases such as *Yersinia pestis*, the plague pathogen. Furthermore, it is not only possible to identify if an individual had the disease but also, with genome level analysis, to look at the history and evolution of plague and infectious diseases in general. The analytical work done on the human remains has, therefore, not just informed about the history of the plague in London but will have far-reaching impact on international studies of plague and its developments in today's world.

The analysis requires relatively small samples of the teeth. With the current site, the analysis was undertaken using samples from the teeth of 20 individuals. This work was undertaken by the Max Planck Institute in Jena, Germany.

The teeth can also be used for isotope analysis on the levels of strontium and oxygen. This can provide information on the geology and water local to an individual, indicating where they came from. Such analysis can potentially identify migrants within a burial population. Carbon and nitrogen isotopes can provide information on variations in diet, nutritional levels and indicators as to general health and stress.

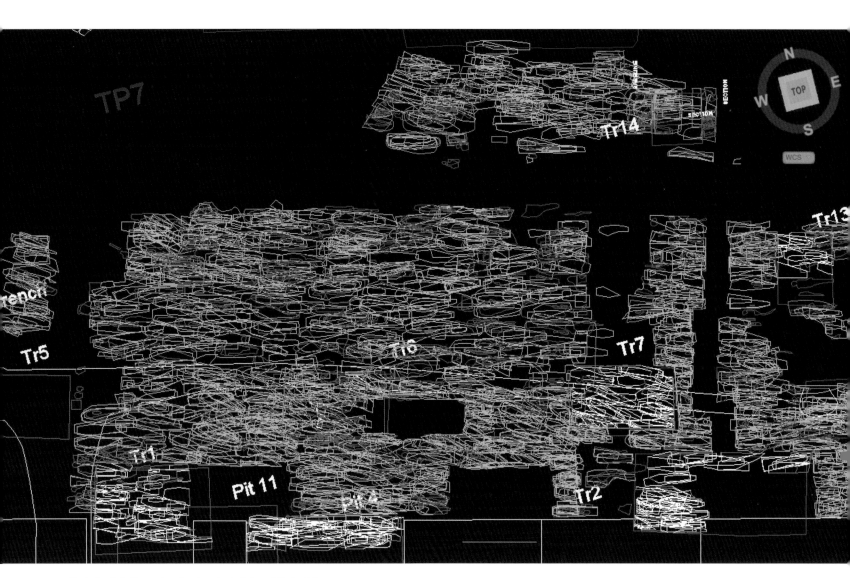

Part of a digitally-produced archaeological plan of the burials
in the main part of the excavation. It shows the density of the
burials in the New Churchyard. The blank areas are those that
were not excavated or where the archaeology did not survive.

The site at Liverpool Street during the excavation of the New Churchyard.

Late 17th to 19th century developments

From 1635 to 1740 the Clitherow family managed the New Churchyard. This meant that they benefitted from any charges for grave digging or for burial vaults.

They also held other jobs, such as ivory or bone turner. In 1707 Benjamin Clitherow converted the ground floor of the family home into a shop. This was one of a number of local shops that made and sold wood, bone and ivory turned items, such as needle cases and handles.

The foundations of the Clitherows' shop and other buildings were found by archaeologists in the south west corner of the burial ground, along with large quantities of bone and ivory-working waste. This shows that they were dumping the waste in the burial ground, adjacent to their shop. The quantity of waste, and the presence of glass-working waste, indicates they may also have been offering a waste disposal service to other workshops. The waste indicates that the Clitherows (and probably others in the area) were making turned objects, such as needle cases and bone optical compendiums for use in telescopes, microscopes and other lenses. A trade token of Ephraim Clitherow's, innkeeper of the Sun Alehouse at Sun Street and Lamb Alley, to the north of the site, was also found. It dates to c. 1648–73.

Two cesspits were excavated relating to properties on Brokers Row, now Blomfield Street, an area well-known for furniture manufacturing and dealing. Both cesspits had been filled in with household rubbish. The rubbish in one dated broadly to the first half of the 18th century and from the other to broadly the second half of the 18th century. It included pottery and porcelain vessels, glass bottles and wineglasses and clay tobacco pipes. A gold Portuguese coin was also found dating to 1721.

In 1823 Liverpool Street was created over the southern part of the burial ground and in 1863-65 most of the northern part was developed as part of Broad Street station.

Bone offcuts, the waste from the production of turned bone objects.

Archaeologists excavate the building foundations and 18th century cesspits .

CHARTERHOUSE SQUARE AND FARRINGDON

Archaeological investigations took place at Farringdon station as part of the construction of the eastern ticket hall, and at Charterhouse Square, where a grout shaft was dug to help underpin surrounding buildings during construction work.

A team of 20 archaeologists uncovered hundreds of objects, some dating back to medieval and Roman times. The most notable of the medieval discoveries on the project were found here, where analysis of the 14th century burials in the shaft has confirmed the presence of the Black Death, through ancient DNA analysis.

"The excavations in Charterhouse Square for a grout shaft disturbed the remains of a cemetery, founded in 1348 in response to the Black Death."

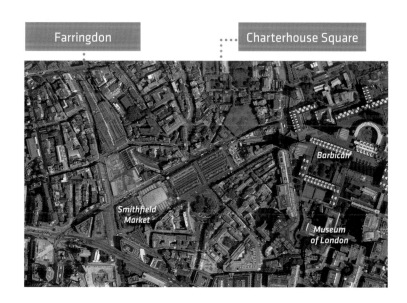

Medieval and post-medieval Charterhouse

A large ditch was excavated to the south of Charterhouse Square. It may be the remains of the Faggeswell Brook which flowed into the Fleet river to the west.

The ditch formed the southern boundary to both the cemetery and the London Charterhouse monastery, which was founded in 1371. Charterhouse monastery was suppressed in 1538 and its buildings were either demolished or adapted to other uses. In 1611 some were converted into the Charterhouse school, which continues to this day at a site in Hertfordshire.

The archaeologists excavated layers of rubbish that had been used to fill in the Faggeswell brook ditch between c 1580 and c 1630-40. Much of it reflects the wealth of the aristocratic houses in this area. Decorated floor tiles probably came from the monastery. They date to the 1300s and were made in Penn, Buckinghamshire.

The damp conditions in the ditch preserved organic material, such as leather and textile. The leather items comprised shoes, pieces of horse harness and part of a possible jerkin, all dating to the late 1500s. The shoes have flat soles, as heels only became common after around 1600. The small fragments of textile include luxury silks produced in Italy and the Spanish empire.

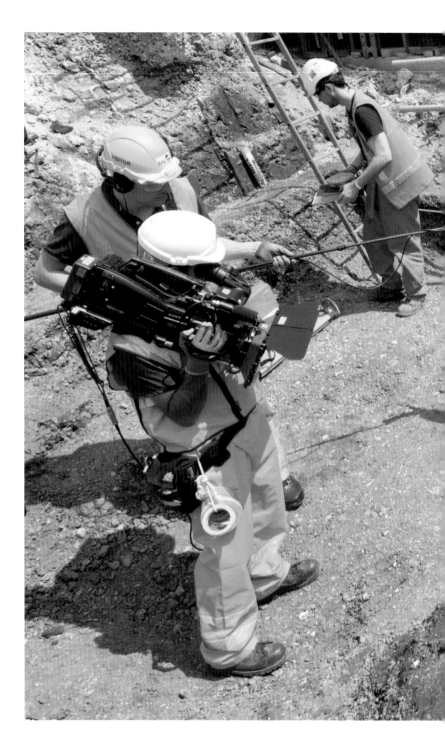

The archaeological excavation at Farringdon. Much of the archaeological work on the Crossrail project was filmed for use both on the Crossrail website and also in a number of documentaries that were made.

Food remains included grape, fig, apple, walnut, coriander and hops. Straw and grass probably came from stabling. The seeds included melegueta pepper, also called 'grains of paradise', a native spice of West Africa. It is an unusual find on archaeological sites, although it was a popular substitute for black pepper in the medieval period.

Imported and locally produced pottery was also found. These included a miniature jug and part of a tankard, made in Cologne and decorated with Venus and the judgement of Paris. Another fragment of stoneware has been shaped into a counter. A near complete tripod pipkin was a more local product, coming from the Surrey-Hampshire borders.

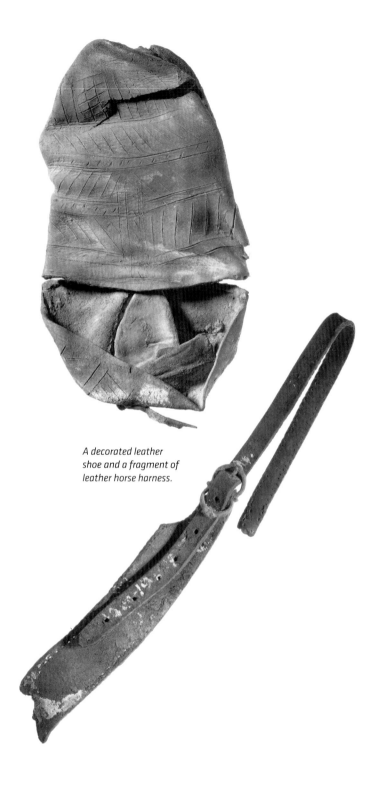

A decorated leather shoe and a fragment of leather horse harness.

The ceramic tripod pipkin made in the Surrey-Hampshire borders.

The Farringdon station eastern ticket hall site with Smithfield Market building in the background.

85

The Charterhouse Square burials

The excavations in Charterhouse Square for a grout shaft disturbed the remains of a cemetery, founded in 1348/9 in response to the Black Death. The plague, or Black Death, was most frequently spread by the bite of infected fleas. It killed 60-70% of the people who caught it. In just two years, between 1348 and 1350, the disease killed around half the population of London.

Twenty-five skeletons were found in three layers at the site. These represent three different phases of burial in the 14th and 15th centuries. All three phases contained skeletons that tested positive for Yersinia pestis (the plague pathogen).

The first phase of burials dated to when the cemetery opened as an emergency Black Death burial ground, with Carthusian Street built as an access route to it. It is not known how many people were buried here in this first phase and estimates vary from over 2,000 to as many as 20,000. Of these 11 were found in the grout shaft. Nine were adult, one adolescent and one child. Yersinia pestis was found in one skeleton. All were buried on the same south-west to north-east alignment, with their heads to the south-west. There was no sign of any grave markers, but the graves were laid out in rows with enough space to walk between them.

GROUT SHAFTS

Grout shafts were excavated to facilitate compensation grouting – a method of stabilising the surrounding ground and buildings. Each shaft is 4.5m in diameter and at the bottom of each pipes were fed out into the surrounding earth, allowing grout to be pumped into the soil. Farringdon was one of five locations on the Crossrail route where grout shafts were used.

The grout shaft during the excavation of the third and final phase of burials dating to the 15th century.

An archaeologist excavates some of the 12 skeletons discovered from the third and final phase of burials, dating to the 15th century. Two of the skeletons from this phase tested positive for Yersinia pestis.

A further phase of burials took place later in the 14th century. This second phase of burials contained two adult males. This phase of the cemetery had been disturbed by later burials. They were buried on the same alignment as the earlier burials. *Yersinia pestis* was found in one skeleton.

The final phase of the cemetery dated to the 15th century and uncovered 12 adult burials. *Yersinia pestis* was found in two of the skeletons. They were all buried on a west-east axis with their heads to the west. Two of the burials were in the same grave and may have been related.

A reconstruction of what the West Smithfield cemetery may have looked like during its first phase. The scene is drawn looking south with St Bartholomew's priory church and St Paul's Cathedral in the background.

Reconstruction drawing by Faith Vardy

Scientific analysis at Charterhouse

As at Liverpool Street, scientific analysis of a number of the individuals buried at Charterhouse was undertaken. Where possible, this included both a DNA and isotopic analysis. Although the sample number is quite small, some amazing details were discovered.

- The presence of Schmorl's nodes on the vertebrae indicates damage to the back due to carrying heavy loads or undertaking strenuous work. This reflects findings at other London medieval cemeteries.

- Many of those tested had rickets which may indicate a poorer population.

- Isotopic analysis of ten individuals indicates that six probably grew up in London and four probably outside of London. Of these, one is likely to be from eastern England, two from central or eastern England, and one from northern England or Scotland. This shows that London in the 14th century was as much a magnet for people from elsewhere as it remains today.

- However, almost all those who had suffered health or nutritional stress in childhood were from London, indicating that life in urban centres was not always a good one.

- The majority of bone fractures occurred amongst those in the final phase of burials in the 15th century. Most fractures were to the ulna, one of the bones in the forearm. These may have been caused by work related or other accidents, such as falls, or by more violent means, such as when parrying a blow by an attacker.

THE FINAL BREAKTHROUGH

The big east-west breakthrough, completing the route, finally happened at 3am on 23 May 2015 when TBM Victoria broke through into the reception chamber at Farringdon's eastern ticket hall, joining together 42 kilometres of tunnels under London.

The expansion of the existing Underground station at Tottenham Court Road and the second ticket hall in Soho, led to major archaeological excavations and the recording of a number of historic buildings before they were demolished.

Further west, eight weeks of investigation of the new ticket halls at Bond Street contributed to our knowledge of the lost rivers of London, long-ago channelled underground and hidden by buildings.

Much of the area to the west of the City of London, what we today call the West End, was largely a rural, farming landscape until the 17th century and so the sites uncovered little in the way of Roman or medieval remains.

"At Tottenham Court Road and Soho a number of buildings were demolished. Perhaps the best known of these was the Astoria music venue, which had previously operated as a theatre and cinema."

Bond Street Station   Tottenham Court Road

Oxford Street

Marble Arch

Crosse and Blackwell

Until the mid-17th century Soho was mainly open fields. Gradually, well-to-do houses were built but by the 19th century the wealthy had moved further west and Soho had become overcrowded and poor.

In the 19th century it was not unusual for large industrial buildings to be located in densely packed residential areas. Edmund Crosse and Thomas Blackwell took over an existing pickle manufacturing firm in Soho in 1830. They relocated to new premises between Soho Square and Charing Cross Road in 1838.

Print showing 20 and 21 Soho Square in 1854. Crosse and Blackwell moved into no. 21 in 1838 and began making fruit preserves from a factory at the back of the property in 1840. They took over no. 20 in 1858.

Photolithograph from a watercolour by Thomas Hosmer Shepherd, (c) Museum of London

Here they manufactured fruit preserves and other commodities. The buildings included kitchens, pickling vaults, offices, bottling and labelling rooms and warehouses. In 1921 the firm moved production from London to Branston in Staffordshire.

The Crosse and Blackwell premises at 151-155 Charing Cross Road, photographed in 1925. It was designed by Robert Lewis Roumieu and opened in 1885.

NO MARGIN FOR ERROR

When tunnelling from Paddington to Farringdon, Tunnel Boring Machine Ada came within 90cm of live Northern line platforms at Tottenham Court Road and within 60cm of passenger escalators, but passed through safely.

An aerial view of the work site at Tottenham Court Road, overlooked by the Centre Point building.

Archaeologists excavate the ceramic and glass vessels from the brick cistern on the site of the Crosse and Blackwell factory.

Over 13,000 vessels were found. They had been dumped in a brick cistern, originally for storing fresh water, when the factory was rebuilt in 1877. All were clean and intact when discarded and some still retained their paper labels. Most are white earthenware pots for potted meat, jam and marmalade and were made by the Maling pottery of Newcastle.

Other vessels included a number of Keiller's marmalade jars, brown stoneware bung jars and bottles, some made in Fulham. The largest amount of glass vessels came from a dump of material under a floor and dates to the early 20th century. Over 4,000 glass stoppers were found as well as cork bungs and other glass and ceramic vessels. Another dump of ceramic and glass vessels to create a new floor surface produced types of vessel not found in the other areas. These also date to the early 20th century and include white ginger jars with blue transfer printed decoration, English stoneware mustard jars and orange-shaped marmalade jars.

A pottery specialist records some of the thousands of vessels recovered from the site.

SOMETHING IN THE AIR

The smell of fruit, boiling sugar and pickling vinegar filled the air around the Crosse and Blackwell factory. In 1840 a visitor commented that 'the smell of fruit pervades everywhere.'

In 1921, following the closure of the factory, a journalist wrote:

'Driving blind-fold through London there are some places that I could always recognise by their distinctive smell. One is the Oxford Street end of Charing Cross Road, where for generations, Crosse and Blackwell's pickle factory has given a very distinctive pungency to the surrounding atmosphere.'

Building recording in Soho

In order to build the new railway, some historic buildings had to be demolished. This happened at several places along the route and in all cases detailed records were made of the buildings before demolition.

Sometimes these records took the form of laser scanning, as at Old Oak Common, but usually it involved detailed surveying and photography of both the interior and exterior of the building. This type of recording is another aspect of archaeological work.

At Tottenham Court Road and this part of Soho a number of buildings were demolished. Perhaps the best known of these was the Astoria music venue, which had previously operated as a cinema and theatre. It had been converted from part of the Crosse and Blackwell warehouse building in 1926-27.

The Bath House, 96 Dean Street.

The building possessed the flamboyant facades, typical of late Victorian pubs, representing the golden age of the public house.

The Astoria

The Astoria at 157-165 Charing Cross Road was one of the most well-known buildings that was demolished in advance of the Crossrail works. It had been converted from the Crosse and Blackwell warehouse that had been built on the site in 1893. The Astoria cinema was designed by Edward A.Stone and opened in 1927, with a dance hall in the basement opening the following year. From 1977 it operated as a theatre, before becoming a live music venue from 1985. It played an iconic role in London's live music scene until its closure in 2009.

The Astoria was demolished that year to make way for the building of the eastern ticket hall for the Elizabeth line Tottenham Court Road station. The remainder of the site will include a retail development and a retail development and theatre.

1. A club flyer promoting six Christmas all-nighters with Fantasy FM at the Astoria, 1991.

2. A poster for the Pakistani film 'Shama', which was released in 1974 and had its London premier at the Astoria in September 1975.

3. Photograph by George Davison Reid, showing the Astoria cinema to the left, early 1930s.

Bond Street and Tyburn

Archaeological excavations in advance of the expansion of Bond Street station uncovered evidence for the now buried Tyburn river when one of its channels was found.

The remains of 18th century building foundations indicated a damp or even water-logged ground surface. This reflects what is already known about the history of this area. Building expansion in the 18th century led to increased management of the Tyburn and its channels. Eventually in 1926 the river was diverted via a series of buried conduits.

The Crossrail project has allowed archaeologists to glimpse a number of the now-disappeared rivers of London. All tributaries of the Thames, some are better known than others; some have almost completely disappeared, whilst others remain, diverted beneath busy roads and basements.

This wooden water pump was found during the excavations. It was used in water management in the area.

Lost London Rivers

The Walbrook

The Walbrook flows south through the City of London and was heavily utilised by the Romans. Becoming increasingly blocked and liable to flooding it was re-dug as the Deep Ditch in the medieval period. From the mid-15th century it began to be culverted and built over. Today nothing of it can be seen, but if you stand at the junction of Queen Street and Cannon Street and look east along Cannon Street, the topography of the Walbrook valley can still be recognised.

The Fleet and the Faggeswell Brook

The Faggeswell Brook is a small tributary of the Fleet, which is itself a tributary of the Thames. The Fleet flows south from its twin sources on Hampstead Heath, entering the Thames just to the west of the City of London. It was long a source of water for a variety of industries, becoming increasingly polluted. It has been culverted since the 19th century. The Faggeswell runs west into the Fleet partly through the Charterhouse site, although its complete route is uncertain.

Hampstead Heath is the source of a number of the lost London rivers

The Tyburn

Rising in Hampstead, the Tyburn is today completely culverted, flowing south below Buckingham Palace and entering the Thames in Pimlico. It is said to be the source of a water feature in the basement of an antiques centre at the junction of Oxford Street and Davies Street. It has long functioned as a boundary and its name comes from the Anglo-Saxon 'boundary stream'.

The Westbourne

Rising at Whitestone Pond in Hampstead, the Westbourne is a small tributary that meanders southwards through Kilburn, Bayswater and Chelsea. It has been known by a number of different names, including the Bayswater, the Serpentine river and the Ranelagh Sewer. Knightsbridge gets its name as one of the crossing points of the Westbourne. Since the 19th century the Westbourne has been redirected to flow through a series of iron pipes.

PADDINGTON TO OLD OAK COMMON

Heading further west, the line runs under Paddington station, coming above ground level at Royal Oak where a new portal was built. From there, the route runs through Westbourne Park and Old Oak Common and then on towards Heathrow and Reading.

The new portal and running lines to the west gave the project the opportunity to uncover more evidence of the prehistory of London, as well as some treasures from its Victorian railway heritage.

"Archaeologists working at Royal Oak discovered evidence of a prehistoric landscape centred on the upper reaches of the lost Westbourne river."

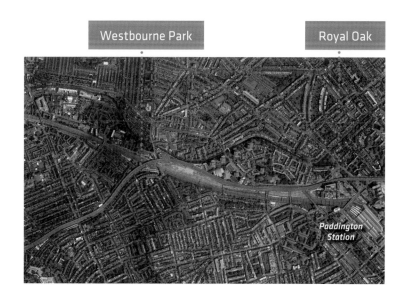

Westbourne Park

Royal Oak

Paddington Station

Reindeer and bison at Royal Oak

Archaeologists working at Royal Oak discovered evidence of a prehistoric landscape centred on the upper reaches of the Westbourne river. The Westbourne once flowed from Hampstead in the north, south to the Thames.

The river channel dates back 68,000 years. Pollen sampling indicates that the valley would then have been open and treeless, dominated by grasses and herbs. The dating of the channel was by Optically Stimulated Luminescence (OSL). About 100 fragments of large mammal bones were recovered and have been identified as bison and reindeer. They date to the late Pleistocene era. Marks on three of the bison bones show that they were gnawed by carnivores, such as wolves and bears.

(Above) An archaeologist at work at the Royal Oak site.

(Right) Crossrail construction at Westbourne Park and Royal Oak Portal. The site of the Westbourne Park depot was sandwiched between the Grand Junction Canal (to the left in the image) and the GWR track. Today it is dominated by the A40 Westway.

Scientific analysis at Royal Oak

The dating of the channel was by Optically Stimulated Luminescence (OSL) undertaken by the University of Wales Trinity Saint David, Lampeter. They worked closely with curators at the Natural History Museum, who identified the large mammal bones and undertook microscopic analysis of the bones' surfaces to identify wear, gnawing and other marks. The bones have been donated to the Natural History Museum.

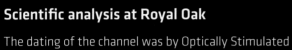

Westbourne Park Depot: Brunel structures

One of the most interesting discoveries of the Crossrail project was the uncovering of structures associated with the early expansion of the railways. In 1833 Isambard Kingdom Brunel (right) was appointed chief engineer to the Great Western Railway (GWR), which ran from London to Bristol.

The GWR London terminus was Paddington, which opened in 1838. It was replaced in 1854 with a building designed by Brunel. This new, larger station meant the engine sheds and workshops had to move and a field in Westbourne Park was developed for this purpose. Here train engines were brought to be serviced and worked on. Archaeologists uncovered the remains of workshops, turntables and a 200 metre-long (663 foot) engine shed. The latter was built for the company's broad-gauge locomotives and later modified to take the standard gauge. Brunel and his chief engineer Daniel Gooch had decided to use a broad gauge (2140mm) for the GWR as it was wider and could carry more freight. After Brunel's death in 1859 the standard gauge (1435mm) was gradually adopted. It is still used in Britain today.

The vast engine shed contained four inspection pits, one is shown here. The excavation showed how the width of the pits was narrowed from broad to standard gauge by the addition of a brick skin to each side wall of the pit.

This cast iron manhole cover was found during the excavations at the Westbourne Park depot. It is embossed 'GWR' and 'OIL' and 'GAS'.

The Westbourne Park Depot was added to and modified over time, often in response to technological changes on the railways. This 40 foot diameter turntable was enlarged to 55 foot and 6 inches in 1896. It was abandoned in 1907.

Old Oak Common

By the end of the 19th century, Paddington and its associated goods yards and depots at Westbourne Park and elsewhere, were stretched to capacity and further expansion was needed.

In 1899 a strip of land at Old Oak Common was identified as suitable for a new depot. When it opened in 1906 it was described as the largest in Great Britain, if not the world.

The depot included a vast engine shed measuring 444ft by 360ft. It contained four turntables for moving rolling stock and was able to accommodate 112 locomotives. It was largely demolished in 1963, after the introduction of double-cab diesel engines made the need for turntables redundant.

Parts of the depot continued in use until 2009 when it was closed in advance of the Crossrail project works. Recognising the importance of the site in terms of railway heritage, where possible, items were retained for re-use. A 1903 cast iron column has been preserved for incorporation into the new Crossrail depot that will occupy the site.

An isometric laser-scan of Old Oak Common's repair shop and lifting bay.

The lifting shop at Old Oak Common in use. The photograph probably dates to shortly after the depot opened in 1906.

Art Deco-style teacups and saucer fragments, dating from the 1920s to the early 1940s, with the GWR logo, were found at the site. They were made for use in the GWR Great Western Hotel at Paddington station. They were robust and designed for frequent use.

111

DELIVERING IT SUSTAINABLY

Throughout the project sustainability has been more than just a buzzword. Crossrail has endeavoured to reuse, recycle or donate unwanted machinery, infrastructure and even earth. From four tonnes of bricks from the manor at Stepney Green that were donated to English Heritage for restoring Britain's Tudor buildings, to over three million tonnes of earth that helped create the RSPB reserve at Wallasea, the achievements have been remarkable.

More than seven million tonnes of soil, rocks and other material were removed during construction, and over 98% was reused. Most of the soil went to helping develop the Wallasea Island Wild Coast nature reserve, but some also went to create new farm or industrial land, as well as other nature reserves and recreational sites.

Along the route, historic building materials were earmarked for reuse wherever possible. Sometimes complete structures were even moved as with the footbridge at North Woolwich. At Connaught Tunnel a pump headhouse was deconstructed for rebuilding elsewhere. At Stepney Green Tudor bricks were donated to English Heritage for restoration works, and at Paddington New Yard, Brunel era bricks went to a heritage railway.

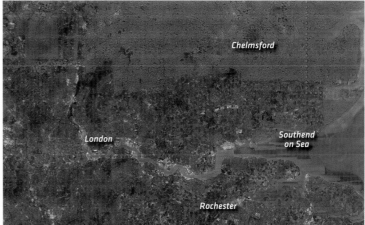

The established Jubilee Marsh on Wallasea Island, Essex

How much material was dug out during the Crossrail project?

More than seven million tonnes of soil, rocks and other material were removed during construction.

Over 98% of it was reused to create new farm or industrial land, as well as nature reserves and recreational sites.

What happened to the tunnel boring machines?

Where possible the TBMs were recycled. Many of their parts were sold around the world to be used in other engineering projects. Parts of Ada and Phyllis were buried where they finished tunnelling near Farringdon as they could not be removed from these sites.

What happens to all the objects?

Tens of thousands of objects were excavated from the Crossrail sites.

With the exception of the amber and early animal bones which have been given to the Natural History Museum, and the heritage construction materials, all the objects, records, images and plans are now part of the Museum of London's Archaeological Archive, where they are available for future research.

Thank you to our sponsor

BFK is a joint venture of BAM, Ferrovial and Kier comprising three of the world's leading rail, tunnelling, and civil engineering companies. As recognised industry leaders in infrastructure projects, they have an established capability in the delivery of complex railway and tunnel projects.

BFK was awarded the C300/C410 and C435 projects including the construction of 6.4 kilometres of twin tunnels Royal Oak Portal - Farringdon, Bond Street and Tottenham Court Road station caverns, ventilation shaft and crossover at Fisher Street, 5 cross passages, East and West Ticket Hall construction at Farringdon Station plus 1.4 kilometres of platform tunnels, cross passages and MEP works.

Credits and acknowledgements

We would like to thank the following for their support and advice during the archaeology programme:
Westminster City Council; The London Charterhouse; Museum of SoHo; Historic England London Team; City of London Department of the Built Environment; Stepney City Farm; London Metropolitan Archives; LAARC; Heritage Railway Association; LURS; McMaster University Ontario; University of Keele; St Giles-in-the-Fields Church; SS Robin Trust; Great Western Railway Society; Thames Ironworks Trust; City of London School for Girls; Carmarthen School of Art; True North Films and Channel 4 TV. Special thanks go to our stakeholders and local community volunteers for their help during the archaeology programme.

In the production of this book we would like to thank the following:
Will Parkes, Jay Carver, Sarah Allen and Marit Leenstra of Crossrail; David Bowsher and colleagues at MOLA (Museum of London Archaeology); Richard Brown and colleagues at Oxford Archaeology, and Simon Parfitt at the Natural History Museum.

All images are © Crossrail, unless otherwise noted, and in particular we would like to acknowledge Andy Chopping and Maggie Cox, MOLA and Gary Evans, Vix Hughes, Andy Shelley and Magda Wachnik, Oxford Archaeology and Daniel Garrity at Crossrail.

Pages 9/21/31/41/45/51/63/81/95/ 105/113 - Google Earth images: © Google

Pages 14/15/16/17 - Maps: © Museum of London

Page 25 - Thames valley water level images: © MOLA

Page 34 - Cleopatra's needle: © National Maritime Museum, Greenwich, London

Page 37 – Film still: BFI National Archive

Illustrated London News illustration: © Museum of London
West Ham badge: © 1895 - 2016 West Ham United Football Club

Page 42 - On the River Lee near Stratford: © The British Library Board. Maps.K.Top.XXVIII.19

Page 43 - Glass bottle and pewter measure: © Museum of London

Page 65- Illustration from Copperplate map of London: © Museum of London

Pages 74-75 - Skeleton photography: © Museum of London

Page 96 - Print showing 20 and 21 Soho Square in 1854. Photolithograph from a watercolour by Thomas Hosmer Shepherd: © Museum of London.

Page 101 - Astoria Theatre: © Ian Newman, The Theatre Trust
Fantasy FM Flier: Courtesy Museum of London
Shama film poster: Courtesy Museum of London
George Davison Reid photograph: © Museum of London

Page 103 - Map: ©2016 Esri, (data providers). All rights reserved. Contains OS data © Crown Copyright and database right 2016.

Page 111 - © Museum of London

Page 114 - Wallasea Island Aerial © RSPB Seal © RSPB

Page 117 - © Museum of London

Tunnel title design by Nissen Richards Studio